ACTIVE
BIBLE STUDIES

BY KURT JOHNSTON & KATIE EDWARDS

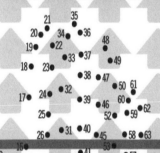

20
EXPERIENCE-DRIVEN
BIBLE STUDIES
FOR JUNIOR HIGHERS

Active Bible Studies
20 Experience-Driven Bible Studies for Junior Highers

Credits
Authors: Kurt Johnston and Katie Edwards
Executive Developer: Nadim Najm
Chief Creative Officer: Joani Schultz
Cover Art Director: Veronica Lucas
Designer: Veronica Lucas
Production Manager: DeAnne Lear

10 9 8 7 6 5 4 3 2 1   17 16 15 14 13 12 11 10 09
Printed in the United States of America.

LETTER FROM THE AUTHORS

Katie and I have been leading junior high small groups for a combined total of over 30 years, and one thing we've noticed is that they are, to say the least, quite active. In a typical junior high small group, students are actively playing video games, jumping on trampolines, eating snacks, flicking each other's ears, laughing, telling stories from their day at school. Yep, junior high small groups are active. Active, that is, until the time to settle down for some Bible study. Unfortunately it's at this precise moment that almost all activity ceases. Eyes glaze over, drool forms in the corners of mouths, and a semi-comatose state seems to infect everybody at the same time. If students do happen to be engaged during Bible study, it's usually not in the Bible study itself, but in some unrecognizable tangent they have wandered down.

We know this to be true because we have experienced it in our own small groups from time to time. That's why we are super excited about *Active Bible Studies*! A couple of years ago we got tired of asking our adult volunteers to deliver dull, un-engaging lessons and decided to do something about it. Ever since then we have been committed to writing Bible studies that set both our leaders and our students up to win. Each lesson in *Active Bible Studies* will actively engage your students in God's Word and will truly make Scripture come to life.

To make the most of *Active Bible Studies*, you may want to:

- **Prepare your students:** You may want to let your kids know ahead of time that you are going to be mixing things up a bit and that to make the most of the lessons they should come with an open heart that is willing to be a bit curious, creative, and cooperative.

- **Plan ahead:** Because most of these lessons require a little bit of forethought and planning, you won't be able to just show up and "wing it."

- **Put your own twist into the mix:** Like any curriculum, *Active Bible Studies* can stand alone but will probably be even more effective if you add a touch or two of your own.

- **Pray:** Ask God to bless your students as you teach these lessons. That's our prayer for you!

Thanks for loving junior highers,

Kurt Johnston & Katie Edwards

TABLE OF
CONTENTS

TABLEOF
CONTENTS

ARMOR OF GOD
LEADER GUIDE

MATERIALS NEEDED

- Big sheets of white paper, poster board, or white wrapping paper
- Markers
- Scissors
- Tape

! WHAT'S THE POINT?

Most of your students won't spend time in the military as adults, but you can still help them discover the importance of defensive armor and offensive weapons in their spiritual lives. This lesson gives you a chance to teach them about being protected and prepared to stand their ground for God.

Start with the Word

Read Ephesians 6:10-20 (NLT)

A final word: Be strong in the Lord and in his mighty power. Put on all of God's armor so that you will be able to stand firm against all strategies of the devil. For we are not fighting against flesh-and-blood enemies, but against evil rulers and authorities of the unseen world, against mighty powers in this dark world, and against evil spirits in the heavenly places. Therefore, put on every piece of God's armor so you will be able to resist the enemy in the time of evil. Then after the battle you will still be standing firm.

Stand your ground, putting on the belt of truth and the body armor of God's righteousness. For shoes, put on the peace that comes from the Good News so that you will be fully prepared. In addition to all of these, hold up the shield of faith to stop the fiery arrows of the devil. Put on salvation as your helmet, and take the sword of the Spirit, which is the word of God.

Pray in the Spirit at all times and on every occasion. Stay alert and be persistent in your prayers for all believers everywhere. And pray for me, too. Ask God to give me the right words so I can boldly explain God's mysterious plan that the Good News is for Jews and Gentiles alike. I am in chains now, still preaching this message as God's ambassador. So pray that I will keep on speaking boldly for him, as I should.

GROUP ACTIVITY

Divide your students into groups of two or three. Give each group the assignment to construct the different elements of the Armor of God. Give each group paper, markers, scissors, and tape. As the students create each piece, they need to outfit one of the group members in the armor. After the construction is complete, have each group give their explanations for each piece of the armor.

Student Instructions
- Divide into groups of two or three.
- Use the materials given to create and construct your own version of the Armor of God.
- Each element that you design must incorporate what the actual piece of armor is and what it represents.
- You can use words, drawings, pictures, etc. to illustrate your armor.
- As you construct your armor, fill in the student sheet provided.
- After you construct all of the armor, you must dress one of your team members in the armor and teach the other teams about what you created.

START A DIALOGUE

As your students are working on the construction of their armor, ask some simple questions to start discussion. You can ask these to individual students or ask the whole group.

- What do you think that "element" of the armor is all about?
- What does the word "faith" mean to you?
- Why do you think this passage is an important one to study?
- Why do you think salvation is the helmet?
- Who do you think we as believers need to stand our ground against?
- What is the good news? Why is there peace in the good news?
- Do you believe that you are prepared to stand firm in your faith?
- In verse 16 it talks about fiery arrows; what does that mean to you?

HOW DOES THIS APPLY?

- What areas of the armor do you need to better understand?
- How can the "armor" be real in your life?
- Do you think that if you were faced with opposition you could stand firm?
- Why do you think it is important for you to know and understand these six pieces of our faith?

TAKE-HOME CHALLENGE

- Read Ephesians 6:19-20.
- In this passage, Paul asks for prayer; why?
- What is Paul's mission?
- Bring back the answers next week!

ARMOR OF GOD
STUDENT HANDOUT

Read Ephesians 6:10-20 (NLT)
A final word: Be strong in the Lord and in his mighty power. Put on all of God's armor so that you will be able to stand firm against all strategies of the devil. For we are not fighting against flesh-and-blood enemies, but against evil rulers and authorities of the unseen world, against mighty powers in this dark world, and against evil spirits in the heavenly places. Therefore, put on every piece of God's armor so you will be able to resist the enemy in the time of evil. Then after the battle you will still be standing firm.

Stand your ground, putting on the belt of truth and the body armor of God's righteousness. For shoes, put on the peace that comes from the Good News so that you will be fully prepared. In addition to all of these, hold up the shield of faith to stop the fiery arrows of the devil. Put on salvation as your helmet, and take the sword of the Spirit, which is the word of God.

Pray in the Spirit at all times and on every occasion. Stay alert and be persistent in your prayers for all believers everywhere. And pray for me, too. Ask God to give me the right words so I can boldly explain God's mysterious plan that the Good News is for Jews and Gentiles alike. I am in chains now, still preaching this message as God's ambassador. So pray that I will keep on speaking boldly for him, as I should.

Armor #1: _____
What is this piece used for?

Armor #2: _____
What is this piece used for?

Armor #3: _____
What is this piece used for?

Armor #4: _____
What is this piece used for?

Armor #5: _____
What is this piece used for?

Armor #6: _____
What is this piece used for?

 TAKE-HOME CHALLENGE

Read Ephesians 6:19-20
In this passage, Paul asks for prayer. Why? What is Paul's mission?
Bring back the answers next week!

EXPERIENCING TIME WITH GOD
LEADER GUIDE

MATERIALS NEEDED

- Boom box, iPod, laptop – something that plays music
- Worship CDs
- Paper
- Pens, markers, pencils

WHAT'S THE POINT?

It is so important for students to begin the habit of spending time with God daily. This lesson is designed to expose students to what spending time with God each day could look like. It is an opportunity for students to experience a variety of practical ways to worship God on their own.

Start with the Word

Read Romans 12:1-2 (NLT)
And so, dear brothers and sisters, I plead with you to give your bodies to God because of all he has done for you. Let them be a living and holy sacrifice—the kind he will find acceptable. This is truly the way to worship him. Don't copy the behavior and customs of this world, but let God transform you into a new person by changing the way you think. Then you will learn to know God's will for you, which is good and pleasing and perfect.

Read Mark 12:30 (NLT)
"Love the Lord your God with all your heart and with all your soul and with all your mind and with all your strength."

- Who or what has the biggest influence on your life?
- Do you feel like the "world" or your culture shapes most of your thoughts, or does God shape most of your thoughts?
- How often do you connect with God now?
- What does that connection time look like?
- Are there any obstacles in your life that keep you from connecting with God?

GROUP ACTIVITY

Expose your students to different ways to experience time with God. Choose as many of the following activities as you would like and go in any order. You can help them focus on one or two, or give them samples from all of the areas listed below. All activities can be experienced together. After you complete each individual exercise ask the activity follow-up questions.

Student Instructions
Experience #1: Listen to this song

> **Leader:** Choose any song from a worship CD and listen to the song together.
>
> **One step further:** Have your group sing along to the same song. Provide the words and see what happens. This could be awkward in some settings, but it also could be very powerful in the right setting.
>
> **Activity Follow-up Questions**
> - What did you hear?
> - How did this song make you feel?
> - What point was the artist trying to communicate?
> - What did this song make you think about?
> - Is there a passage in the Bible that is associated with this song?

Experience #2: Be silent and listen to God for two minutes

Leader: Instruct your students to sit still and be completely quiet for two minutes. Keep time.

Activity Follow-up Questions
- Does complete silence make you uncomfortable?
- How often do you come before the Lord in silence?
- How can silence on your part be a good thing in your relationship with God?

Experience #3: Spend 10 minutes with God

Leader: Walk your students through a guided prayer time. You are giving them the opportunity to experience a 10-minute prayer time with God. Keep time and give instructions along the way.

Leader: Take a moment and read the "Lord's Prayer" in Matthew 6. It's a great passage to read as you prepare for this lesson.

Pray for one minute – Thank God for who He is and what He has done for you
Pray for three minutes – Confess any sin in your life; lay it down before God
Pray for three minutes – Ask God for what you need
Pray for two minutes – Bring requests before God on behalf of others in your life
Pray for one minute – Surrender to God and His will for you

Activity Follow-up Questions
- Did the 10 minutes go by fast?
- How often do you spend a focused time of prayer with God?
- Do you think you could try to pray for 10 minutes a day?

Experience #4: Read and study the following passage

Leader: Choose any passage that you want to study as a group. Then, work students through the list of questions below.

Study Tips for Students
- Highlight or underline key words
- Who are the main characters?
- Where does this take place?
- Highlight or underline a key verse or a key phrase
- Are there any terms you don't understand?
- Does this verse speak to you?
- Does it have any relevance for your life right now?
- Stop and reflect on this passage for one minute

Activity Follow-up Questions
- How often do you read and study God's Word?
- Do you have a particular study method you use?
- Did the questions above help you understand this passage better?

Experience #5: Draw a picture or pictures while you are listening

Leader: Read a passage or play a song. Instruct students to draw on the backside of their student sheet, or give them a separate sheet. Choose any passage or any song and have your student simply draw what they hear.

Example Passage: Psalm 100
¹Shout with joy to the LORD, all the earth!
²Worship the LORD with gladness. Come before him, singing with joy.
³Acknowledge that the LORD is God! He made us, and we are his. We are his people, the sheep of his pasture.
⁴Enter his gates with thanksgiving; go into his courts with praise. Give thanks to him and praise his name.
⁵For the LORD is good. His unfailing love continues forever, and his faithfulness continues to each generation.

Activity Follow-up Questions
- What did you draw?
- What did this passage/song make you think about?

Leader: Don't make students share if they want to; they may have drawn something that they don't feel comfortable sharing with the group.

Experience #6: Create your own station!

? HOW DOES THIS APPLY?

- Why is it important to connect with God as often as possible?
- Do you think God wants to connect with you?
- What do you think is the result of connecting with God each day?
- Do you feel closer to God after tonight's activity?

▲▲ TAKE-HOME CHALLENGE

- Can you make a commitment to try to connect once a day with God?
- Fill out the six-day commitment on your student sheet and fill in what you are going to try to do this week to connect with God.

EXPERIENCING TIME WITH GOD
STUDENT HANDOUT

Read Romans 12:1-2 (NLT)
And so, dear brothers and sisters, I plead with you to give your bodies to God because of all he has done for you. Let them be a living and holy sacrifice—the kind he will find acceptable. This is truly the way to worship him. Don't copy the behavior and customs of this world, but let God transform you into a new person by changing the way you think. Then you will learn to know God's will for you, which is good and pleasing and perfect.

Read Mark 12:30 (NLT)
"Love the Lord your God with all your heart and with all your soul and with all your mind and with all your strength."

Experience #1:

Experience #2:

Experience #3:

Experience #4:

Six-Day Commitment
Write down how you are going to connect with God each day

Day #1:

Day #2:

Day #3:

Day #4:

Day #5:

Day #6:

GET BELOW THE SURFACE
LEADER GUIDE

MATERIALS NEEDED

- As a leader, bring four personal items that describe you
- Give your students instructions one week prior to this lesson

WHAT'S THE POINT?

This lesson is designed for you and your students to get below the surface and begin knowing each other on a deeper level.

Start with the Word

Read Ecclesiastes 4:9-12 (NLT)

Two people are better off than one, for they can help each other succeed. If one person falls, the other can reach out and help. But someone who falls alone is in real trouble. Likewise, two people lying close together can keep each other warm. But how can one be warm alone? A person standing alone can be attacked and defeated, but two can stand back-to-back and conquer. Three are even better, for a triple-braided cord is not easily broken.

Leader Note: This passage illustrates the types of relationships that we want to build with our fellow believers in Christ. However, to achieve the kind of relationship highlighted in this passage of Ecclesiastes, we need to get to a place where we truly know and trust one another. True friendship and fellowship take time to build. Today can be a first step for your students.

Every student needs to bring four items to your small group time. When your group comes together each person in your small group will share their items with the group.

Student Instructions

> **Leader Note: Communicate a week before you teach this lesson**
>
> Next week you need to bring four items that represent the different areas of your life. It can be a picture, an object, or anything else. For example, if you are a soccer player and that is a big part of your life, you might bring a picture of your soccer team or your favorite soccer ball. You can bring in any item that represents the four categories below.
>
> - Bring one item that represents your personality
> - Bring one item that tells us what your family is like
> - Bring one item that describes your favorite thing to do
> - Bring one item that represents your relationship with God/your spiritual life
>
> **Leader Note:** Depending on your students, you might need to give some practical examples.
>
> **Leader Note: On the night of your group**
>
> Circle your students up and discuss one category at a time. Allow each student to share their items in each category. Encourage your students to ask questions about each other's items.
>
> - Share your item that represents your personality
> - Share your item that tells us what your family is like
> - Share your item that describes your favorite thing to do
> - Share your item that represents your relationship with God/your spiritual life
>
> **Leader Note:** Have each student write down the items of the other people in their group on their student sheet.

HOW DOES THIS APPLY?

- How can you get to know the people in this group on a deeper level?
- Does knowing the answers to these questions inspire you to know the person more?
- Why is it important to know the people in your small group?
- Does knowing more about the people in your group help you trust them more?

TAKE-HOME CHALLENGE

This week, what is one way you could encourage or support another student in the group?

GET BELOW THE SURFACE
STUDENT HANDOUT

Read Ecclesiastes 4:9-12
Two people are better off than one, for they can help each other succeed. If one person falls, the other can reach out and help. But someone who falls alone is in real trouble. Likewise, two people lying close together can keep each other warm. But how can one be warm alone? A person standing alone can be attacked and defeated, but two can stand back-to-back and conquer. Three are even better, for a triple-braided cord is not easily broken.

Group Member #1 _____
Items Shared:

Group Member #2 _____
Items Shared:

Group Member #3 _____
Items Shared:

Group Member #4 _____
Items Shared:

Group Member #5 _____
Items Shared:

Group Member #6 _____
Items Shared:

Group Member #7 _____
Items Shared:

Group Member #8 _____
Items Shared:

Group Member #9 _____
Items Shared:

Group Member #10 _____
Items Shared:

 TAKE-HOME CHALLENGE

What is one way this week that you could encourage or support another student in the group?

I am going to commit to encouraging...

GOD'S VIEW VS. THE WORLD'S VIEW [GIRLS ONLY]
LEADER GUIDE

MATERIALS NEEDED

- A giant stack of magazines (variety of magazines)
- Construction paper
- Glue sticks or tape
- Markers

WHAT'S THE POINT?

Most junior high girls struggle with how they perceive themselves. This lesson is designed for each girl to take an honest look at how the world sees her and how God sees her.

Start with the Word

The World's View...
You are not good enough. You don't have enough. You don't have what it takes to succeed. You don't look right. You need

_____.

God's View...
Read Psalm 139:13-18
You made all the delicate, inner parts of my body and knit me together in my mother's womb. Thank you for making me so wonderfully complex! Your workmanship is marvelous—how well I know it. You watched me as I was being formed in utter seclusion, as I was woven together in the dark of the womb. You saw me before I was born. Every day of my life was recorded in your book. Every moment was laid out before a single day had passed. How precious are your thoughts about me, O God! They are

innumerable! I can't even count them; they outnumber the grains of sand! And when I wake up in the morning, you are still with me!

GROUP ACTIVITY

Give each girl a piece of paper. Have her write her name at the top of the paper on both sides. Then, on one side of the paper have her write "God's View" and on the other side of the paper have her write "The World's View." Place the stack of magazines, scissors, glue sticks, and other items in the middle of your circle. Have the girls clip articles, pictures, word phrases, and letters that illustrate each side.

Student Instructions
- Write your name at the top of your paper on both sides
- On one side write "God's View" and on the other side write "The World's View"
- Create a collage by cutting out pictures, words, letters, and phrases that illustrate how the world sees you
- Flip over the other side and create a collage by cutting out pictures, letters, words, and phrases that illustrate how God sees you
- Write out Psalm 139:13-18 on the side that reads "God's View"

START A DIALOGUE

Leader Note: Begin this discussion while the students are creating their collages
- What do you think "the world" or our culture wants you to be?
- How does the world want you to dress, act, talk, and behave?
- Do you care how you look all of the time?
- What do you think God wants you to be?
- Why do you think God created all of us uniquely?

- Do think you are trying too hard in your daily life to live up to the world's expectations?
- Can you admit that God created you to be a masterpiece?
- What are some ways that you could learn to love who God created you to be?

TAKE-HOME CHALLENGE

Tape up your collage in a spot in your room where you will see it daily. Make sure you can see the side that says "God's View" as a reminder of how God sees you and what you were intended for.

GOD'S VIEW VS. THE WORLD'S VIEW [GIRLS ONLY]
STUDENT HANDOUT

Read Psalm 139:13-18

You made all the delicate, inner parts of my body and knit me together in my mother's womb. Thank you for making me so wonderfully complex! Your workmanship is marvelous—how well I know it. You watched me as I was being formed in utter seclusion, as I was woven together in the dark of the womb. You saw me before I was born. Every day of my life was recorded in your book. Every moment was laid out before a single day had passed. How precious are your thoughts about me, O God! They are innumerable! I can't even count them; they outnumber the grains of sand! And when I wake up in the morning, you are still with me!

LOCAL & GLOBAL MISSIONS
LEADER GUIDE

 MATERIALS NEEDED

Leader Note: This requires you to gather some materials ahead of time; most items and information can easily be found in local stores or on the Internet.
- Push pins
- Tape
- Paper
- Miscellaneous items; see list below

 WHAT'S THE POINT?

Often times, there is a misperception that "missions" only refers to a trip halfway around the world. However, there are "missions" opportunities everywhere, including our own backyard. This lesson is designed to expose students to that fact that all Christians are called to do missions – and that calling does not always requires us to get on a plane to fulfill it. We can experience and fulfill our call to missions simply by being aware of local and global needs and responding. This lesson is an opportunity to expose your students to local and global missions.

Start with the Word

Read "The Great Commandment" in Matthew 22:37-39 (NLT)
"Love the Lord your God with all of your heart and with all of your soul and with all of your mind. This is the first and greatest commandment. And the second is like it: love your neighbor as yourself."

Read "The Great Commission" in Matthew 28:19-20 (NLT)

"Therefore, go and make disciples of all the nations, baptizing them in the name of the Father and the Son and the Holy Spirit. Teach these new disciples to obey all the commands I have given you. And be sure of this: I am with you always, even to the end of the age."

A Definition of Missions

Missions is ENGAGING where the gospel and local church are not accessible. It is carrying out the Great Commandment and the Great Commission locally and globally by every Christian in the world.

> **Local Missions:** Carrying out the Great Commandment and the Great Commission in your surrounding community.

> **Global Missions:** Carrying out the Great Commandment and the Great Commission in any area that is outside your local community.

> **If we are going to respond to Jesus' call to missions, where do we start?**

GROUP ACTIVITY

Create a room full of individual stations that students rotate through for three minutes at a time. The stations do not need to be secluded from one another; they just need a little distance. Any size room can work. Get creative with your space!

Below is a list of possible station ideas. **You do not need to use all of them**. You simply choose the ones that work best for your students and your setting. Some of the stations require some materials. Try to borrow these items instead of buying them.

Station #1: Pray for the world

Find a poster-size world map. You can typically find them at a local bookstore, or ask a teacher if you can borrow one for a night. Hang it up on the wall and place the push pins next to it.

Instructions: Choose a country on the map. Mark it with a push pin. Write down the country you chose on your paper. Take a moment and pray for that country.

Things to pray for:
- Pray for the leadership in that country to make good choices
- Pray for the people's immediate needs to be met
- Pray for people who aren't Christians; pray that they will come to know Jesus Christ personally

Station #2: Make a donation

Create a list of donation needs for any of your local shelters, food banks, senior homes, non-profit organizations, or other groups meeting people's needs. Post a typed list of these groups for the students to see at the station. Give your students as many donation ideas as you want!

Instructions: Choose an item from the donation list that you would be willing to donate. Write down the donation item or items of your choice and commit to donating it. You don't have to choose just one! Challenge yourself!

Station #3: Pray for your community

Find a small map of your local area/community. Hang it up on the wall and place a box of push pins next to it.

Instructions: Choose an area on the map of your local community. Mark it with a push pin. Write down the area you chose on your paper. Take a moment and pray for that part of your community.

Things to pray for:
- Pray that God will open a door for you to reach non-Christians in that area
- Pray that people will know Jesus in a deeper way
- Pray that people will come to church and be a part of your church family

Station #4: Something small can do something big

Post the attached list of "25 Ways to Use a Dollar." This station is designed to illustrate that students can make an impact on someone's life for Jesus Christ with something as small as a dollar. Let them know that by doing something small they allow God to open a door for questions and conversations.

Leader Note: You can take this a step further by giving each student a real dollar and encouraging them to put this idea into action this next week.

> **Instructions:** Did you know that something small can make an impact for Jesus Christ? Did you know that something as small as a dollar can open up a door for you to talk to someone about Jesus? Whether you are in another country or in your community – choose one of these ideas to make an impact on someone. Commit to making one of these ideas happen…and when the person asks why you did what you did, tell them why!

Station #5: Pray for a child

Go to a website that has a "child support" program available. Print out pictures of kids from different countries and place them at the station.

> **Instructions:** Choose a picture of a child. Write the child's name down on your paper. Take a moment and pray for this child.

> **Things to pray for:**
> - Pray for the child's physical needs to be met: food, water, shelter, clothing, education, a care taker, etc.
> - Pray that this child will come to know Jesus Christ personally
> - Pray that someone will support this child on an ongoing basis

Station #6: How can I get involved?

Create a list of different local and global missions opportunities in your church that students can consider. Be sure to list opportunities that are open to students in your church setting.

> **Instructions:** Choose an item on this list that you might want to investigate further. Write down the opportunity on your paper. During this rotation ask your leader how you can get more involved.

Station #7: What's in your room?

Students have a variety of simple items that can be an excellent donation for local organizations.

> **Instructions:** What is in your room? Do you have any clothes that don't fit anymore? Do you have any toys that are in good condition that you could part with? Do you have shoes that you have outgrown? Take a moment to think about your bedroom. Are there any items that you would consider donating to a local organization in need? Write down any items you think of on your paper.

Station #8: Create your own station that exposes students to missions

Leader Note: Give students some ownership in this lesson and have them investigate a new idea that is not listed. If you have Internet access maybe you could work with them to find one!

> ### Instructions
> - Spend three minutes at each station around the room
> - No talking; this is your time to think, pray, and reflect
> - Use your student sheet to record your thoughts at ` each station
> - Listen for your leader's voice to tell you when to rotate to the next station
> - After you have completed every station come back to meet with the group in the center of the room

START A DIALOGUE

As your students move from station to station try asking...
What did you think of that last station?

HOW DOES THIS APPLY?

- What station did your heart connect with most?
- Was there a station that you feel like you might want to be connected to regularly?
- What do these items make you think about?
- Do you have a better understanding of some of the ways you can get involved in missions?

TAKE-HOME CHALLENGE

Take the dollar challenge this week and report back next week!

LOCAL & GLOBAL MISSIONS
STUDENT HANDOUT

Read Matthew 28:19-20 (NLT)
"Therefore, go and make disciples of all the nations, baptizing them in the name of the Father and the Son and the Holy Spirit. Teach these new disciples to obey all the commands I have given you. And be sure of this: I am with you always, even to the end of the age."

Read Matthew 22:37-39
"Love the Lord your God with all of your heart and with all of your soul and with all of your mind. This is the first and greatest commandment. And the second is like it: love your neighbor as yourself."

Station #1

Station #2

Station #3

Station #4

Station #5

Station #6

Take the dollar challenge this week and report back next week!

A LETTER TO THE PHILIPPIANS
LEADER GUIDE

 MATERIALS NEEDED

- Pens or markers
- Paper
- Envelopes

 **WHAT'S THE POINT?**

This lesson is designed to give students a glimpse of Paul's insights and his ministry. Help students understand that to live is Christ, and to live for Christ means to share Christ with all who are around you and to encourage those who know Christ to do the same. This is also an opportunity to go through a book of the Bible as a group.

Start with the Word
Read the book of Philippians together as a group.

> **Verses to highlight along the way...**

Chapter 1	**Chapter 3**
Philippians 1:16	Philippians 3:7-8
Philippians 1:29-30	Philippians 3:13-14
Chapter 2	**Chapter 4**
Philippians 2:5-11	Philippians 4:4
Philippians 2:14-15	Philippians 4:6-7
	Philippians 4:13

Break up your students into groups of two or three. Assign each group a chapter of Philippians. Have them write a letter to "the Philippians." Allow each group to define who "the Philippians" are. It may be a school, a group of friends, a team, your youth group, or some other group of people. This is going to vary from group to group. Explain that Paul's letter to the Philippians was meant to encourage and inspire people toward following Christ daily. Encourage your students to look at what Paul wrote and then try to write a letter of their own.

Student Instructions
- As a group read your assigned chapter of Philippians
- Together pick out the highlights, key verses, key phrases, and other important ideas
- Put yourself in Paul's shoes and write a letter to "the Philippians"
- Your group can define who "the Philippians" are; it may be a school, a group of friends, a team, your youth group, or some other group of people
- Use the themes from your chapter to help you figure out what to write
- Make it personal and specific to your "Philippians"
- Write down the themes for each chapter on your student sheet

Main themes:
Chapter 1 – God is at work in our lives
Chapter 2 – Check your heart; check your attitude
Chapter 3 – Put the past behind you
Chapter 4 – Having a joyful attitude

- What are some of the main ideas that Paul was trying to communicate to the Philippians?
- Did you try to communicate the same ideas to your "Philippians"?
- Does Paul's letter encourage you in your walk with Jesus Christ?
- Do you think your letter could encourage someone in their walk with Christ?

TAKE-HOME CHALLENGE

Write a letter to someone speaking of the joy that Christ brings to your life and encouraging them in their walk with Christ, and then send it!

A LETTER TO THE PHILIPPIANS
STUDENT HANDOUT

**Read the book of Philippians
Chapters 1-4**

Group 1 / Chapter 1
Who are the Philippians?

Letter Highlights:

Group 2 / Chapter 2
Who are the Philippians?

Letter Highlights:

Group 3 / Chapter 3
Who are the Philippians?

Letter Highlights:

Group 4 / Chapter 4
Who are the Philippians?

Letter Highlights:

 TAKE-HOME CHALLENGE

Write a letter to someone speaking of the joy that Christ brings to your life and encouraging them in their walk with Christ, and then send it!

SHHHHH! THE POWER OF ACTIONS OVER WORDS
LEADER GUIDE

MATERIALS NEEDED

The materials will vary from group to group depending on what you want to do for this activity.

WHAT'S THE POINT?

This lesson is based on the quote from St. Francis of Assisi: "Preach the gospel at all times and when necessary use words."

Remind students that being a follower of Christ requires us to talk the talk, and walk the walk. Our actions can speak just as loudly as our words, and sometimes they can be a little louder.

HANDS-ON ACTIVITY

As each student enters your small group hand them the student sheet and instruct them not to talk. The purpose of this lesson is to teach students that actions can make a huge impact on their non-Christian friends. Students are communicating their faith through the way they act, the way they use their body language, the way they react, and the way they respond with their facial expressions. Spend the first 20 minutes of your small group time doing things in silence. Students will need to use their actions to communicate. You as the leader can speak and give instruction during this time.

Silent activity ideas
- Have students greet one another using no sound
- Eat a snack together; ask how the snack tastes and ask them to encourage the person who made the snack

- Play a silent game; charades is an easy silent game, but be sure your students express everything in silence
- Pray for one another; have them put a hand on the shoulder of the person they are praying for

Leader Note: Ask students to communicate using only actions within each of these activities. If they have a question, encourage them to ask it using facial expressions, movement, etc.

Student Instructions

Welcome to small group. Tonight we are going to start our group in a different way. For the first 20 minutes you are not allowed to use your voice. No talking. Complete silence. If you need to communicate something, you need to communicate through your actions.

 START A DIALOGUE

- Do you think actions can speak louder than words?
- What types of actions speak loudly?
- What does the following quote from St. Francis of Assisi mean to you: "Preach the gospel at all times and when necessary use words"?
- How can you communicate your love for Christ to others through your actions?
- Do you think people know you are a Christ-follower by the way you act?
- What are some ways that we can preach God's Word without actually saying a word?
- Why is it important for our actions to match our words?
- Are there people in your life that do not know you personally and only know you on actions alone? Do they know you are a Christian?

Go to the Word

Read John 13:34-35 (NLT):

"So now I am giving you a new commandment: Love each other. Just as I have loved you, you should love each other. Your love for one another will prove to the world that you are my disciples."

- According to this passage what is one way that we can show the world that we are Christ-followers?

Read Colossians 4:5 (NLT):

Live wisely among those who are not believers, and make the most of every opportunity. Let your conversation be gracious and attractive so that you will have the right response for everyone.

- Why do you think this tells us to be wise in the way you act with people who are not believers?

 HOW DOES THIS APPLY?

- What type of impact do you think you could have on a non-believer's life if your actions spoke loudly?
- What kind of impression do you leave on your non-Christian friends when you act negatively?

 TAKE-HOME CHALLENGE

Write down the names of three people you know who do NOT know Jesus Christ. Think about the way you act around them; are you preaching the gospel with your actions? Is there anything you can change in the way you act around them? Is there something you can do this week to communicate Christ's love to those three people just using your actions?

SHHHHH! THE POWER OF ACTIONS OVER WORDS
STUDENT HANDOUT

"Preach the gospel at all times and when necessary use words."
- St. Francis of Assisi

Read John 13:34-35 (NLT)
"So now I am giving you a new commandment: Love each other. Just as I have loved you, you should love each other. Your love for one another will prove to the world that you are my disciples."

Read Colossians 4:5 (NLT)
Live wisely among those who are not believers, and make the most of every opportunity. Let your conversation be gracious and attractive so that you will have the right response for everyone.

 TAKE-HOME CHALLENGE

Write down the names of three people you know who do NOT know Jesus Christ. Think about the way you act around them; are you preaching the gospel with your actions? Is there anything you can change in the way you act around them? Is there something you can do this week to communicate Christ's love to those three people just using your actions?

My Three Friends

_____

_____

_____

BOARD GAME
LEADER GUIDE

MATERIALS NEEDED

- Large white poster board (enough for two-person teams to have one board)
- Markers; a variety of colors
- Small objects that can be used as game pieces
- Colored paper

WHAT'S THE POINT?

This offers a creative approach to exposing students to some different events and people in the Old Testament.

Start with the Word
- Moses and the Red Sea
- Israelites going to the Promised Land
- David vs. Goliath
- The walls of Jericho
- Shadrach, Mesach, and Abednago
- A Psalm
- Noah
- Gideon
- Adam and Eve

  Leader Note: Add any passages that you think might interest your students

Divide your group into teams of two. Have each team choose a passage/story from your list and create a board game for the other students in your group to play.

Student Instructions

- Create a board game using the white poster board and a passage from your leader's list.
- Each team needs to choose a different passage.
- Create a game board, game pieces, rules, rewards, etc.
- It needs to be a game for two to four players.
- You need to incorporate as many elements of your passage as possible. You are not allowed to change any elements of the story to fit your game. It must be accurate.
- It's your game, so be creative; it can be as simple or as complicated as you want it to be.
- Once you have completed your game, you will need to present and teach your game/passage to the rest of the group. Each group also needs to come up with an application for their passage. How can this passage from the Bible relate to the lives of your fellow group members?
- Then, as a group we will take turns playing one another's games.
- Remember: A board game is typically a journey including a start, obstacles, rewards, and a final destination.

  Leader Note: This lesson could last a couple of weeks depending on how creative and detailed your students get.

START A DIALOGUE

As students begin creating their board games:
- Assist them in choosing a passage
- Help them understand the different points of their passages
- Ask questions, give suggestions, help them figure out the progression of their game, etc.

HOW DOES THIS APPLY?

Each group should come up with their own application for their chosen passage. As leaders, you might want to remind them of this as they choose and create their game.

TAKE-HOME CHALLENGE

Write a summary of all of the passages shared.

ONCE UPON A PARABLE
LEADER GUIDE

 **MATERIALS NEEDED**

This will vary group to group depending on the parable chosen.

! **WHAT'S THE POINT?**

Expose students to Jesus' storytelling technique. Teach them the ways that Jesus used parables to illustrate God's Word and put things into the terms of the people He was trying to reach.

Start with the Word
Choose one parable from the list below to read together. Before you read the parable take a moment to define what a parable is for your students.
- Good Samaritan – Luke 10:25-37
- Good shepherd – John 10:1-18
- Laborers in the vineyard – Matthew 20:1-16
- Lost coin – Luke 15:8-10
- Lost sheep – Luke 15:4-7
- Prodigal son – Luke 15:11-32
- Ten minas – Luke 19:11-27
- The sower – Luke 8:4-15

Definition of Parable
A parable is an earthly story with a heavenly meaning.

GROUP ACTIVITY

Divide your students into groups of two or three and assign each group a parable. Have each group read the parable and then come up with a re-enactment of the parable.

Student Instructions

- Together as a group read the parable assigned to you
- Figure out the setting, the characters, and what lesson Jesus was trying to teach
- Put together a re-enactment of this parable for the other students in your group
- As you act out the parable be sure to communicate the main points that Jesus was trying to communicate

START A DIALOGUE

Leader Note: After each re-enactment, ask these questions

- Why do you think Jesus taught this parable?
- Who was the main audience in the Bible for this parable?
- Why do you think Jesus chose storytelling to get His teachings heard?
- Does this parable apply today? How?
- How would you re-tell this parable to your peers? Would you change the setting and story?

HOW DOES THIS APPLY?

- What illustrations or stories have you told to get a point across to others?
- Are there stories that we can tell that can illustrate living a Christ-centered life?

Write a parable of your own. Choose a lesson or a promise from the Bible and write a story that will illustrate the main points. Try telling it to a friend this week.

ONCE UPON A PARABLE
STUDENT HANDOUT

My Parable:

Main Characters:

Main Points:

Group #1
Parable:

Main Characters:

Main Points:

Group #2
Parable:

Main Characters:

Main Points:

Group #3
Parable:

Main Characters:

Main Points:

Group #4
Parable:

Main Characters:

Main Points:

 TAKE-HOME CHALLENGE

Write a parable of your own. Choose a lesson or a promise from God's Word and write a story that will illustrate the main points. Try telling it to a friend this week.

A NOT-SO-RANDOM ACT OF KINDNESS
LEADER GUIDE

 MATERIALS NEEDED

- Note cards/small gifts
- Ingredients for chocolate chip cookies
- More time than usual
- Paper plates
- Clear cello wrap or foil
- Have parents contribute
- Allow yourself some travel time

 WHAT'S THE POINT?

Some people underestimate how compassionate junior highers can be. In this lesson, your students will discover some simple, practical ways to demonstrate God's love and kindness to the world around them.

Start with the Word

Read Matthew 5:43-48

"You have heard the law that says, 'Love your neighbor' and hate your enemy. But I say, love your enemies! Pray for those who persecute you! In that way, you will be acting as true children of your Father in heaven. For he gives his sunlight to both the evil and the good, and he sends rain on the just and the unjust alike. If you love only those who love you, what reward is there for that? Even corrupt tax collectors do that much. If you are kind only to your friends, how are you different from anyone else? Even pagans do that. But you are to be perfect, even as your Father in heaven is perfect.

HANDS-ON ACTIVITY

Everyone in the group chooses one person for an act of kindness.

- Have each student choose someone that they would like to do something for – someone in their life in need of kindness.
- This person can be an acquaintance, a friend, or a complete stranger.
- Challenge them to choose someone who they believe would really benefit from this kindness. (Encourage them to avoid picking best friends, immediate family, etc.)
- Assemble small packages of kindness, with note cards, plates of chocolate chip cookies, and other items.
- Begin assembling small gifts for each person that has been chosen; make a plate of chocolate chip cookies, a note card, and whatever else for each person. Make it personal and really encouraging.
- Get in the car and deliver each gift; do this together as a group or send everyone out and have them report back next week.

Student Instructions

- Choose a person in your life for a not-so-random act of kindness
- Try to choose someone you really believe to be in NEED of kindness
- Assemble a small encouragement card/gift
- Make it encouraging and personal
- When you have completed it, give it away!

START A DIALOGUE

- Why did you choose this particular person? Why are they in need of kindness?
- How would you feel if someone took the time to do something for you?
- Why is it important to demonstrate kindness and love toward each other?

- What would our world look like if everyone did one act of kindness per day?
- What is challenging about being kind?

HOW DOES THIS APPLY?

- Do you think something as simple as an act of kindness can point someone toward Jesus Christ?
- Do you think your act of kindness will open up any doors to talk to that person about Christ?

TAKE-HOME CHALLENGE

Try to do one act of kindness per day for the next week.

A NOT-SO-RANDOM ACT OF KINDNESS
STUDENT HANDOUT

Read Matthew 5:43-48

"You have heard the law that says, 'Love your neighbor' and hate your enemy. But I say, love your enemies! Pray for those who persecute you! In that way, you will be acting as true children of your Father in heaven. For he gives his sunlight to both the evil and the good, and he sends rain on the just and the unjust alike. If you love only those who love you, what reward is there for that? Even corrupt tax collectors do that much. If you are kind only to your friends, how are you different from anyone else? Even pagans do that. But you are to be perfect, even as your Father in heaven is perfect.

PRAY FOR ONE ANOTHER
LEADER GUIDE

 **MATERIALS NEEDED**

- A black marker
- White paper
- Tape
- Stereo

! WHAT'S THE POINT?

This lesson is designed to get your students praying for one another. This is a great opportunity to push them out of their comfort zone and really challenge them in their prayer life. This lesson can go in so many directions – praying for one another, the power of prayer, etc.

Start with the Word

Read James 5:13-16
"Is any one of you in trouble? He should pray. Is anyone happy? Let him sing songs of praise. Is any one of you sick? He should call the elders of the church to pray over him and anoint him with oil in the name of the Lord. And the prayer offered in faith will make the sick person well; the Lord will raise him up. If he has sinned, he will be forgiven. Therefore confess your sins to each other and pray for each other so that you may be healed. The prayer of a righteous man is powerful and effective."

START A DIALOGUE

- Do you think prayer is a powerful tool?
- Why do we pray?
- Have you seen God work through prayer?
- Have you ever prayed for something that God did not give you?
- Are you still waiting for an answer to prayer?

GROUP ACTIVITY

Create prayer stations around the room for your students to rotate through, two minutes at a time. Give each student a student sheet, a blank white sheet of paper, and a black marker. Each student will write his or her name on the white paper, along with his or her prayer requests. Then, have students tape their sheets in different spots around the room. Finally, have students spend two minutes at each paper praying for the requests listed. Instruct them to switch spots every two minutes. Play some soft worship music to create the right atmosphere.

Student Instructions

- Write your name in big letters at the top of your white paper
- Below your name write your prayer requests; you can write as many as you would like
- Your list can include your own needs or the needs of others in your life
- Tape your sheet up on the wall somewhere around the room
- Before you begin rotating through the stations take a minute and work through the first three items on your student sheet
- Take your student sheet and walk around the room and pray for each group member for two minutes
- Write down any prayer requests that you would like to continue to pray for during the week

- This is a silent activity; this is a time for you to lift these requests to God in prayer, so try to focus

  Leader Note: Remind students that these prayer requests should be kept private within the group.

Before your students begin rotating through the stations, have them take a moment to prepare their hearts. These steps are listed on their student sheet.
- Step #1 Take a moment and praise God for who He is
- Step #2 Take a moment and confess any sin you have in your life to God
- Step #3 Take a moment and surrender your heart to God

 HOW DOES THIS APPLY?

- Why is it important to go to God in prayer on a regular basis?
- Why do we pray for others?
- How does it make you feel to know someone is praying for you?

TAKE-HOME CHALLENGE

Pray for one group member each day of the next week. Use your student sheet to help you remember specific requests. Before you pray for your friends take a moment to prepare your heart. Walk through steps 1 through 3 at the top of your student sheet before you begin praying.

PRAY FOR ONE ANOTHER
STUDENT HANDOUT

Read James 5:13-16

"Is any one of you in trouble? He should pray. Is anyone happy? Let him sing songs of praise. Is any one of you sick? He should call the elders of the church to pray over him and anoint him with oil in the name of the Lord. And the prayer offered in faith will make the sick person well; the Lord will raise him up. If he has sinned, he will be forgiven. Therefore confess your sins to each other and pray for each other so that you may be healed. The prayer of a righteous man is powerful and effective."

Before you start, take a moment to prepare your heart:
- Step #1 Take a moment and praise God for who He is
- Step #2 Take a moment and confess any sin you have in your life to God
- Step #3 Take a moment and surrender your heart to God

Station #1
> Group Member:
> Prayer Request:

Station #2
> Group Member:
> Prayer Request:

Station #3
> Group Member:
> Prayer Request:

Station #4

Group Member:
Prayer Request:

Station #5

Group Member:
Prayer Request:

Station #6

Group Member:
Prayer Request:

Station #7

Group Member:
Prayer Request:

Station #8

Group Member:
Prayer Request:

 TAKE-HOME CHALLENGE

Pray for one group member each day of the next week. Use your student sheet to help you remember specific requests. Before you pray for your friends take a moment to prepare your heart. Walk through steps 1 through 3 at the top of this sheet before you begin praying.

THE LAST DAYS OF JESUS
LEADER GUIDE

MATERIALS NEEDED

- Large plastic eggs (two per student)
- Candy
- Marker
- Communion supplies (optional; depends on your setting)

WHAT'S THE POINT?

The object of this activity is to spend some walking through the last days of Jesus' life and then to spend some time reflecting on what Jesus Christ did for each of us.

Start with the Word

Read Luke 22, 23, 24:1-8

GROUP ACTIVITY

Take time to encourage one another as a group by creating an encouragement note that keeps on giving throughout the week.

Leader Instructions
- Buy two large plastic eggs for each student in your group.
- Label the plastic eggs with each student's name and a number
- Avoid giving students two numbers that are close together. For example, you might assign numbers as Nicole 1, Nicole 12, Katie 3, Katie 8.

- Print out the passages in Luke. Cut it into parts and number the separate pieces of the passage.
- You need two slips of paper per student in your group. Be sure to cut the passage so you don't have any leftover Scripture.
- Put candy and a slip of paper in each egg. Be sure the number on the passage paper corresponds with the number of the egg. These numbers determine how you will read the passage aloud together.
- Hide the eggs.
- Have each student find their eggs and bring them to the circle; they can't open their eggs until their number is called.
- OPTION: When you get to the egg that contains the Last Supper, take communion together (or take communion at the end).

Student Instructions
- Find the eggs with your name on it
- When you find them bring them back to the circle
- Do NOT open your eggs until your number is called
- Read the passage your egg contains; keep the candy

 START A DIALOGUE

Spend some time talking after each egg is opened. Have your students read the passages twice. Walk them through the meanings of each passage. Talk about the events that are happening. Allow them to ask any questions they might have. It's okay if you don't have all of the answers!

? HOW DOES THIS APPLY?

- Do you understand what took place and why?
- What do Jesus' death and resurrection mean to you?
- What does it mean for the world?
- When was the last time you told someone about what Jesus Christ did for us?

Tell someone why we celebrate Easter. Use the Scripture that we studied today to help you account for what happened and why.

THE LAST DAYS OF JESUS
STUDENT GUIDE

Read Luke 22, 23, 24:1-8
Write down key words or thoughts from the passages in each Easter Egg.

Egg #1
What passage is it?
What is the main idea in this passage?
Underline the people in this passage.
Underline the places listed in this passage.

Egg #2
What passage is it?
What is the main idea in this passage?
Underline the people in this passage.
Underline the places listed in this passage.

Egg #3
What passage is it?
What is the main idea in this passage?
Underline the people in this passage.
Underline the places listed in this passage.

Egg #4
What passage is it?
What is the main idea in this passage?
Underline the people in this passage.
Underline the places listed in this passage.

Egg #5
What passage is it?
What is the main idea in this passage?
Underline the people in this passage.
Underline the places listed in this passage.

Egg #6

What passage is it? _____
What is the main idea in this passage?
Underline the people in this passage.
Underline the places listed in this passage.

Egg #7

What passage is it? _____
What is the main idea in this passage?
Underline the people in this passage.
Underline the places listed in this passage.

Egg #8

What passage is it? _____
What is the main idea in this passage?
Underline the people in this passage.
Underline the places listed in this passage.

Egg #9

What passage is it? _____
What is the main idea in this passage?
Underline the people in this passage.
Underline the places listed in this passage.

Egg #10

What passage is it? _____
What is the main idea in this passage?
Underline the people in this passage.
Underline the places listed in this passage.

TAKE-HOME CHALLENGE

Tell someone why we celebrate Easter. Use the Scripture that we studied today to help you account for what happened and why.

ENCOURAGEMENT JAR
LEADER GUIDE

 **MATERIALS NEEDED**

- Medium-size Mason jars
- Black marker
- Decorations (optional)
- Small pieces of colored paper

 **WHAT'S THE POINT?**

Every day we are burdened by negative stuff in our lives. This lesson is designed to talk about encouraging one another and lifting each other up instead of tearing one another down.

Start with the Word

Read John 13:34-35
"A new command I give you: Love one another. As I have loved you, so you must love one another. By this all men will know that you are my disciples, if you love one another."

 **GROUP ACTIVITY**

Take time to encourage one another as a group by creating an encouragement note that keeps on giving throughout the week.

Leader Instructions
- Give each student a Mason jar.
- The student can either decorate it or just write their name in marker on the side of the jar or on the lid.
- Give each student a stack of small colored pieces of paper.

- Have each student write encouraging thoughts, notes, and verses to the other students in your group. Everybody has to do at least one for each jar/student, and then they can add extras to each jar.
- If you have a student absent from the group, be sure to include a jar for him or her.
- When the exercise is over, students are left with a jar full of encouraging notes that they can open throughout their week.

Leader Note: Because there is no student sheet for this lesson, write the theme verse for this lesson on a piece of paper and place it in each jar.

Student Instructions
- Write your name and/or decorate your Mason jar.
- Take stack of little pieces of colored paper.
- On the colored papers write encouraging thoughts, notes, and verses for each of the other students in your group. Everybody has to do at least one for each jar/student, and then you can add extras to each jar.

 START A DIALOGUE

- How does encouragement affect you?
- How can negative words affect you?
- Have you seen the effects of negative words in your life or someone else's life?

? HOW DOES THIS APPLY?

- Can encouragement or love be life-changing?
- How important is it for non-believers to see Christians loving one another?

Try to write an encouragement note to someone outside of your group. Think of a family member, a friend at school, or a teacher.

POWER UP [GEARED FOR GUYS]
LEADER GUIDE

MATERIALS NEEDED

- A variety of power tools and their non-power counterparts (a power fan and a hand fan, a blender and a wooden spoon, a washing machine and a bucket of soapy water, a power air compressor and a regular tire pump, etc. Get creative!
- A station set up for each tool with a task to perform.
- A stopwatch and pen and paper
- Adult supervision at each station! (Great opportunity to get parents involved in your group for one night.)

WHAT'S THE POINT?

For most junior high boys, living out their faith in Christ is much more difficult than it needs to be. The reason for this is because most junior highers are trying to live life on their own power and forget that as Christians, they have the power of the Holy Spirit within them. This lesson will encourage your junior high boys to allow God's Spirit to give them the power to live for Christ on a daily basis.

Start with the Word

Read Acts 1:8
But you will receive power when the Holy Spirit comes upon you. And you will be my witnesses, telling people about me everywhere—in Jerusalem, throughout Judea, in Samaria, and to the ends of the earth.

Read 2 Corinthians 1:21-22

It is God who enables us, along with you, to stand firm for Christ. He has commissioned us, and he has identified us as his own by placing the Holy Spirit in our hearts as the first installment that guarantees everything he has promised us.

Read Galatians 5:16

So I say, let the Holy Spirit guide your lives. Then you won't be doing what your sinful nature craves.

 **GROUP ACTIVITY**

As a group, move from station to station. At each station give each boy in the group the chance to see how quickly he can accomplish the task, first using the power tool and then doing it by hand. Record the scores for each guy. When you have gone through all the stations, add up each boy's cumulative score and pronounce a winner. If you want, you can award a "power winner" and a "non-power winner."

Leader Preparation
- Create four or five "Power Up" stations
- At each station put one power tool and its manual counterpart (examples above)
- Create a short task that can be performed for each set of tools
- Create a score sheet at each station so students can record their scores
- Rotate students through each station giving them a chance to try each tool and then have them record their score
- Parent or adult supervision is suggested

Student Instructions
- After each station, jot down your thoughts about that activity.
- Why was it always easier to use the power tool instead of doing it by hand?

- How much more frustrating was it when you were trying to do the exact same task without the same power you had at first?

START A DIALOGUE

Leader Note: Start this dialogue while the students are at the last station and continue it when you circle up together.
- What would the world be like with no power?
- What would you think of somebody who refused to do a job using the power tool even though it was available?

HOW DOES THIS APPLY?

- According to the verses we read earlier, what is one of the primary roles of the Holy Spirit in the life of a Christian?
- How often do you "plug into" the power of the Holy Spirit to help you live out your faith in Jesus?
- Can you think of some examples in a junior high guy's life where he might need the power of the Holy Spirit to do what's right?

TAKE-HOME CHALLENGE

If you are a Christian, you have God's Spirit living within you. Unfortunately most junior high boys forget to "power up" and "plug into" the power that the Holy Spirit provides. Instead, they try to tackle the struggles and temptations of junior high on their own strength.

Each morning you may consider a simple prayer like this: "God, I recognize that I have Your Holy Spirit living within me and I know that I'm going to face stuff today that I can't handle on my own. Right now, I want to plug into You and ask that the power of Your Holy Spirit would give me the strength to live for You. Amen."

POWER UP [GEARED FOR GUYS]
STUDENT HANDOUT

Read Acts 1:8
But you will receive power when the Holy Spirit comes upon you. And you will be my witnesses, telling people about me everywhere—in Jerusalem, throughout Judea, in Samaria, and to the ends of the earth.

Read 2 Corinthians 1:21-22
It is God who enables us, along with you, to stand firm for Christ. He has commissioned us, and he has identified us as his own by placing the Holy Spirit in our hearts as the first installment that guarantees everything he has promised us.

Read Galatians 5:16
So I say, let the Holy Spirit guide your lives. Then you won't be doing what your sinful nature craves.

Station #1
My "Power" Score:

My "Manual" Score:

Station #2
My "Power" Score:

My "Manual" Score:

Station #3
My "Power" Score:

My "Manual" Score:

Station #4
My "Power" Score:

My "Manual" Score:

Station #5
My "Power" Score:

My "Manual" Score:

 TAKE-HOME CHALLENGE

If you are a Christian, you have God's Spirit living within you. Unfortunately most junior high boys forget to "power up" and "plug into" the power that the Holy Spirit provides. Instead, they try to tackle the struggles and temptations of junior high on their own strength.

Each morning you may consider a simple prayer like this: "God, I recognize that I have Your Holy Spirit living within me and I know that I'm going to face stuff today that I can't handle on my own. Right now, I want to plug into You and ask that the power of Your Holy Spirit would give me the strength to live for You. Amen."

PICTURE PERFECT
LEADER GUIDE

MATERIALS NEEDED

- Disposable or digital camera
- Eight random pictures of people, places, things, or anything else (read below to see how you will use them; it might help you choose the pictures)
- White paper or poster board (one per student)
- Markers or crayons

WHAT'S THE POINT?

This is lesson is designed to give students "pictures of Jesus." These will be pictures of His character, pictures of the way He loves, and pictures of who He wants to be in our lives. This lesson is divided into three parts and may take longer than one week.

GROUP ACTIVITY

Part 1: SAY CHEESE!

Leader Instructions
Use the disposable camera to take pictures of your students. Be goofy and have fun! If you have a digital camera, show your students the picture after you take each one, and then send them an email during the week with the pictures attached. If you have a disposable camera, get the pictures developed and bring them to your next meeting.

1. Take a picture of all of your students together smiling and looking happy.
2. Divide into groups of two or three. Take a picture of the leader(s) with each group.

3. Take a picture of the two oldest students in your group.
4. Take a picture of the two youngest students in your group.
5. Take a picture of all of the students "in the middle."
6. Take a picture of all of your students posing like gladiators or warriors.
7. Have all of your students sitting in a circle or bunched up together. Stand on a chair and take an aerial shot.
8. Take an action shot. For instance: Everyone jumping in the air at once or jumping off the chairs.
9. Take a picture of the whole group with serious faces, no smiling.
10. Take a picture of the whole group with goofy faces.
11. Create a picture of your own or have your students come up with a creative shot.

Part 2: PICTURE STORY

Leader Instructions
Take out the eight random pictures you brought. Start this exercise by asking the general questions listed below. Then, hold up each individual picture and ask the individual picture questions listed below. Watch the clock; this part of the exercise could maximize your time.

General Questions
- Why do we take pictures?
- How does a picture help us learn about something or someone?
- Can a picture make an impact?
- Can a picture make you feel something?

Individual Picture (Ask these questions for as many of the pictures as you can)
- What story do you think this picture tells?
- What do you think the photographer wanted us to know?

Look at the Word
Read John 14:6
Jesus answered, "I am the way and the truth and the life. No one comes to the Father except through me."

Part 3: THE PICTURE OF JESUS

Leader Instructions
You have been given a list of "Pictures of Jesus" in the Bible. Assign one of the passages listed below to each of your students. Have each student look up the Bible verse and find the word picture of Jesus. Using the paper and the crayons provided. Instruct each student to draw his or her interpretation of that word picture. Once everyone has completed this, have your students share that picture.

Leader Note: Feel the freedom to add to the passages below.

Thoughts to share with your students
God's Word is FULL of pictures that illustrate who Jesus Christ is and who He wants to be in our lives. Just like the pictures we took of each other and the pictures we just looked at, the Bible tell us the story of God's never-ending love for us.

Assign the passages below. Do not reveal the picture; see if your students can pick it out themselves.

Pictures of Jesus
- Isaiah 9:6 (Wonderful Counselor)
- Isaiah 9:6 (Prince of Peace)
- Matthew 11:19 (Friend)
- Matthew 12:18 (Servant)
- John 1:1 (The Word)
- John 1:29 (Lamb of God)
- John 4:42 (Savior)
- John 6:35 (Bread of life)
- John 8:12 (Light of the world)
- John 10:9 (The door)
- John 10:11 (Good shepherd)

- John 14:6 (The way)
- John 14:6 (The truth)
- John 14:6 (The life)
- John 15:1 (The true vine)

HOW DOES THIS APPLY?

- Did these "pictures" teach you something new about Jesus?
- How do these word pictures tell us more about who Jesus is?
- How do these word pictures make you feel about who Jesus wants to be in your life?

TAKE-HOME CHALLENGE

Are there other "pictures of Jesus" in the Bible? Over the next week read your Bible and try to discover new pictures of Jesus that we did not talk about today.

PICTURE PERFECT
STUDENT HANDOUT

Read John 14:6

Jesus answered, "I am the way and the truth and the life. No one comes to the Father except through me."

What pictures of Jesus do you see in the following passages?

- Isaiah 9:6

- Isaiah 9:6

- Matthew 11:19

- Matthew 12:18

- John 1:1

- John 1:29

- John 4:42

- John 6:35

- John 8:12

- John 10:9

- John 10:11

- John 14:6

- John 14:6

- John 14:6

- John 15:1

 TAKE-HOME CHALLENGE

Are there other "pictures of Jesus" in the Bible? Over the next week read your Bible and try to discover new pictures of Jesus that we did not talk about today.

GOD'S VIEW VS. THE WORLD'S VIEW [GUYS ONLY]
LEADER GUIDE

MATERIALS NEEDED

- A giant stack of magazines (variety of surf, skate, sports, and celebrity magazines)
- Construction paper
- Glue sticks or tape
- Markers

WHAT'S THE POINT?

Most junior high guys are trying to figure themselves out. Common questions are "who am I?" or "who should I try to be?" This lesson is designed to help each guy take an honest look at how the world sees him and to compare that with how God sees him.

Start with the Word

The World's View...
You are not good enough. You don't have enough. You don't have what it takes to succeed. You don't look right. You need (fill in the blank…)

God's View...
Read Psalm 139:13-18 (NLT) out loud
You made all the delicate, inner parts of my body and knit me together in my mother's womb. Thank you for making me so wonderfully complex! Your workmanship is marvelous—how well I know it. You watched me as I was being formed in utter seclusion, as I was woven together in the dark of the womb. You

saw me before I was born. Every day of my life was recorded in your book. Every moment was laid out before a single day had passed. How precious are your thoughts about me, O GOD! They are innumerable! I can't even count them; they outnumber the grains of sand! And when I wake up in the morning, you are still with me!

GROUP ACTIVITY

Give each guy a piece of paper. Have him write his name at the top of the paper on both sides. Then, on one side of the paper have him write "God's View" and on other side of the paper have him write "The World's View." Place the stack of magazines, scissors, glue sticks, and other items in the middle of your circle. Have the guys clip articles, pictures, word phrases, and letters that illustrate each side.

Student Instructions

- Write your name at the top of your paper on both sides
- On one side write "God's View" and one the other side write "The World's View"
- Create a collage by cutting out pictures, words, letters, and phrases that illustrates how the world sees you
- Flip over the other side and create a collage by cutting out pictures, letters, words, and phrases that illustrates how God sees you
- Write out Psalm 139:13-18 on the side that reads "God's View"

START A DIALOGUE

Begin this discussion while the students are creating their collages.

- What do you think "the world" or our culture wants you to be?
- How does the world want you to dress, act, talk, and behave?
- Do you feel a lot of pressure to look a certain way, act a certain way, or "be" a certain way to fit in?

- What do you think God would say about the pressure you feel?
- Why do you think God created all of us different?

❓ HOW DOES THIS APPLY?

- Do think you are trying too hard in your daily life to live up to the world's expectations?
- Is it easy or hard for you to recognize that God created you as a custom masterpiece?
- What are some ways that you could learn to appreciate how God made you, and some ways to take the pressure off yourself to live up to the world's standards?

⛰ TAKE-HOME CHALLENGE

Tape up your collage in a spot in your room where you will see it daily. Tape up the side that says "God's View" as a reminder of how God sees you and what you were intended for.

GOD'S VIEW VS. THE WORLD'S VIEW [GUYS ONLY]
STUDENT HANDOUT

Read Psalm 139:13-18

You made all the delicate, inner parts of my body and knit me together in my mother's womb. Thank you for making me so wonderfully complex! Your workmanship is marvelous—how well I know it. You watched me as I was being formed in utter seclusion, as I was woven together in the dark of the womb. You saw me before I was born. Every day of my life was recorded in your book. Every moment was laid out before a single day had passed. How precious are your thoughts about me, O God! They are innumerable! I can't even count them; they outnumber the grains of sand! And when I wake up in the morning, you are still with me!

GRAB BAG
LEADER GUIDE

MATERIALS NEEDED

- Large paper bag, gift bag, or box (something that students have to reach into to grab something out)
- See list of "grab bag" ideas below
- Feel the freedom to add or make up your own

WHAT'S THE POINT?

This lesson is designed for you and your group of students to get to know each other on a deeper level. This exercise can be a fun way to unlock some good conversation with your students.

Start with the Word

Read Philippians 2:12 (MSG)
If you've gotten anything at all out of following Christ, if his love has made any difference in your life, if being in a community of the Spirit means anything to you, if you have a heart, if you care— then do me a favor: Agree with each other, love each other, be deep-spirited friends.

GROUP ACTIVITY

Have your students sit in a circle and pass the grab bag around. Give each student a chance to grab something out and answer the corresponding question. The questions attached to each item are listed below.

Leader Instructions

- Fill the grab bag with the 10-12 items listed below. Feel free to add or subtract as many items as you would like.
- Make sure you have at least one item per student in your group.

Suggested Grab Bag Items

- **Hot Wheel** – What is your dream car?
- **Scary picture** – What scares you? Or what is your biggest fear?
- **Barf bag** – What is your best "BARF" story?
- **Christmas light bulb** – Describe your family's Christmas traditions or share your favorite Christmas memory.
- **Cookie** – Share your favorite baked good or treat.
- **Question mark** – If you could ask God one question what would it be?
- **Family photo** – Spend one minute telling us about your family.
- **Pencil** – If you were writing a book what would it be about?
- **Key** – If you were going to unlock a treasure chest with this key, what kind of treasure would you hope to find?
- **Luggage tag** – If you could travel anywhere where would you go?
- **Ticket stub** – If you could play a leading role in a movie what movie would it be, or what type of movie would it be?
- **Dollar bill** – If you could go on a shopping spree in any store what store would you choose?
- **Lemon** – Would you rather eat a lemon or kiss a rat on the face?

 START A DIALOGUE

This should happen during the passing of the grab bag.

- As the bag is passed, and an item is extracted, ask the corresponding question. After the student answers, open the same question up to the rest of your group.
- Let the students keep their items.

• What new things did you learn about each other today?

TAKE-HOME CHALLENGE

Bring a "grab bag" item next week with a question of your own attached. The group can create a new grab bag with your items and questions inside.

GRAB BAG
STUDENT HANDOUT

Read Philippians 2:12 (MSG)
If you've gotten anything at all out of following Christ, if his love has made any difference in your life, if being in a community of the Spirit means anything to you, if you have a heart, if you care— then do me a favor: Agree with each other, love each other, be deep-spirited friends.

GRAB BAG ITEM:

My Friend's Answers:

GRAB BAG ITEM:

My Friend's Answers:

GRAB BAG ITEM:

My Friend's Answers:

GRAB BAG ITEM:

My Friend's Answers:

GRAB BAG ITEM:

My Friend's Answers:

GRAB BAG ITEM:

My Friend's Answers:

GRAB BAG ITEM:

My Friend's Answers:

GRAB BAG ITEM:

My Friend's Answers:

GRAB BAG ITEM:

My Friend's Answers:

GRAB BAG ITEM:

My Friend's Answers:

 TAKE-HOME CHALLENGE

Bring a "grab bag" item next week with a question of your own attached. The group can create a new grab bag with your items and questions inside.

BECOMING GOD'S GIRL
LEADER GUIDE

 MATERIALS NEEDED

- Large pieces of white butcher paper or white wrapping paper (one per girl in your group)
- Markers
- Red, blue, brown, cream, pink, and green paper (one sheet per student)
- Tape or glue sticks
- Scissors (one pair per student)

 WHAT'S THE POINT?

The Bible is filled with analogies and illustrations that help us learn important principles and ideas. This lesson will take something as familiar as the human body and help the girls in your group discover steps they can take to become women of God.

 GROUP ACTIVITY

Each girl in your group is going to create a picture of what she will look like if she leads a life dedicated to being God's girl.

Leader Instructions
- Give each girl in your group a large piece of white butcher paper or white wrapping paper. The paper must be as long as the student is tall.
- Have each girl trace her body on the piece of paper and cut it out.
- Have each girl tape her "body" up on the walls around the room.
- Walk through the six parts of the exercise with the girls. Follow the instructions for each part.

- After you complete the exercise, have your girls take their "bodies" home and hang it somewhere in their room as a reminder.

Student Instructions
- Take a large piece of white butcher paper or white wrapping paper.
- Grab a pair of scissors, one sheet of each colored paper, and markers.
- Trace your body on the piece of paper and cut it out.
- Tape your "body" up on the wall – anywhere in the room.

GROUP EXERCISE
Leaders feel free to modify any of these to fit your group setting or your group's needs. Read through each part together with your students.

Part 1
Take out the pink piece of paper. Draw a heart and cut it out. Tape or glue the heart to your body hanging on the wall.

Key Verse: Matthew 22:37
Jesus replied: "Love the Lord your God with all your heart and with all your soul and with all your mind. This is the first and greatest commandment."

Things to write around your **HEART**:
- The key verse
- "I want to LOVE God with my whole heart"
- "I will give my whole heart to you God"
- Anything that represents the heart to each individual girl
- Color in your heart with a marker. Don't leave any space, as a symbol of giving your whole heart to God.
- Student Sheet Fill-In: "I will use **MY HEART** to become a woman of God by **LOVING GOD** with my **WHOLE HEART**."

Talk to your girls about what it looks like to give your whole heart to God. Talk about the key verse and what it means. Talk about the heart.

Part 2
Take out the blue or brown pieces of paper. Draw your eyes and cut them out. Tape or glue the eyes to your body hanging on the wall.

Key Verse: John 3:16-18
For God so loved the world that he gave his one and only Son, that whoever believes in him shall not perish but have eternal life. For God did not send his Son into the world to condemn the world, but to save the world through him. Whoever believes in him is not condemned, but whoever does not believe stands condemned already because he has not believed in the name of God's one and only Son.

Things to write around your **EYES**:
- The key verse (John 3:16)
- "God so LOVED the world that He sent Jesus"
- "God LOVES and wants to know everyone on a personal level"
- How do you think God "sees" each one of us?
- "God sees everyone as His children"
- Anything else that they want to write
- Student Sheet Fill-In: "I will use **MY EYES** to become a woman of God by **SEEING OTHERS** through **GOD'S EYES**."

 START A DIALOGUE

Talk to your students about how God sees us and how God sees the world. Talk to them about how God sent His Son for us. What does that say about the way God sees us? Talk about the way we need to see others, including loving those who love us and loving those who don't. How can we see others the way God sees them?

Part 3

Take out the red or pink pieces of paper. Draw your lips/mouth and cut them out. Tape or glue the lips/mouth to your body hanging on the wall.

Key Verse: Proverbs 12:19

Truthful lips endure forever, but a lying tongue lasts only a moment.

Proverbs 15:4

The tongue that brings healing is a tree of life, but a deceitful tongue crushes the spirit.

Proverbs 18:8

The words of a gossip are like choice morsels; they go down to a man's inmost parts.

Proverbs 21:23

He who guards his mouth and his tongue keeps himself from calamity.

Things to write around your **LIPS/MOUTH**:
- The key verses
- "I will let my conversations be full of love and compassion"
- "I will speak kind words about those around me"
- "I will try to use my words wisely"
- "I understand that words are powerful"
- Anything else they want to write
- Student Sheet Fill-In: "I will use **MY MOUTH** to become a woman of God by using my mouth to **SPEAK TRUTH** and **LOVE TO OTHERS**."

START A DIALOGUE

Talk about the power of words, gossip, negative speak, and positive speak, and what kind of effect they can have on the people around us.

Part 4

Take out the cream piece of paper. Draw your hands and cut them out. Tape or glue the hands to your body hanging on the wall.

Key Verse: 1 Peter 4:9-11

Offer hospitality to one another without grumbling. Each one should use whatever gift he has received to serve others, faithfully administering God's grace in its various forms. If anyone speaks, he should do it as one speaking the very words of God. If anyone serves, he should do it with the strength God provides, so that in all things God may be praised through Jesus Christ. To him be the glory and the power for ever and ever. Amen.

Things to write around your **HANDS**:
- The key passage (or part of it)
- "I will serve others because I am called to"
- "I will put others first"
- "God will provide the strength for me to serve"
- "I will use my gifts to serve others and to serve God"
- Anything else they want to write
- Student Sheet Fill-In: "I will use **MY HANDS** to become a woman of God by using my hands to **SERVE GOD** by **SERVING OTHERS**."

 **START A DIALOGUE**

Talk about serving God by serving others. Talk about serving people in need. Talk about a life of being "others-centered."

Part 5

Take out the green piece of paper. Draw your feet/shoes and cut them out. Tape or glue the feet/shoes to your body hanging on the wall.

Key Verse: Isaiah 52:7

How beautiful on the mountains are the feet of those who bring good news, who proclaim peace, who bring good tidings, who proclaim salvation.

Things to write around your **FEET**:
- The key verse
- Write the good news; what is it?
- Write the names of five people you would like to share the good news with
- Write five places you would like to go to share the good news
- Anything else they want to write
- Student Sheet Fill-In: "I will use **MY FEET** to become a woman of God by **BRINGING THE GOOD NEWS** to those around me."

 START A DIALOGUE

Talk about the good news; what is it? Why does Jesus want us to share it? Why is it unfair to keep it to ourselves? How can we share it with others?

Part 6
Take out any colored piece of paper. Draw your ears and cut them out. Tape or glue the ears to your body hanging on the wall.

Key Verse: Psalm 46:10
Be still and know that I am God.

Things to write around your **EARS**:
- The key verse
- "I will take time to listen to God"
- "I want to listen to what God has for me"
- "God wants to speak to me"
- Anything else they want to write
- Student Sheet Fill-In: "I will use **MY EARS** to become a woman of God by **BEING STILL** and **LISTENING TO GOD'S VOICE**."

START A DIALOGUE

Sit in silence for a minute while they are doing this portion. How can we listen to God? Does God really speak to us? How? Has God been speaking to you lately?

TAKE-HOME CHALLENGE

Take your "body" home and hang it somewhere in your room (maybe on the back of your door or on your closet). Each day you see it, be reminded of the different parts of your body and how you can use them to be God's girl each day.

BECOMING GOD'S GIRL
STUDENT HANDOUT

Part 1
Key Verse: Matthew 22:37
Jesus replied: "Love the Lord your God with all your heart and with all your soul and with all your mind. This is the first and greatest commandment.

I will use _____ to become a woman of God by _____ with my _____.

Part 2
Key Verse: John 3:16-18
For God so loved the world that he gave his one and only Son, that whoever believes in him shall not perish but have eternal life. For God did not send his Son into the world to condemn the world, but to save the world through him. Whoever believes in him is not condemned, but whoever does not believe stands condemned already because he has not believed in the name of God's one and only Son.

I will use _____ to become a woman of God by _____ _____ through _____.

Part 3
Key Verses: Proverbs
Truthful lips endure forever, but a lying tongue lasts only a moment (Proverbs 12:19).

The tongue that brings healing is a tree of life, but a deceitful tongue crushes the spirit (Proverbs 15:4).

He who guards his mouth and his tongue keeps himself from calamity (Proverbs 18:8).

He who guards his mouth and his tongue keeps himself from calamity (Proverbs 21:23).

I will use _____ to become a woman of God by using my mouth to _____ and _____

Part 4
Key Verse: 1 Peter 4:9-11
Offer hospitality to one another without grumbling. Each one should use whatever gift he has received to serve others, faithfully administering God's grace in its various forms. If anyone speaks, he should do it as one speaking the very words of God. If anyone serves, he should do it with the strength God provides, so that in all things God may be praised through Jesus Christ. To him be the glory and the power for ever and ever. Amen.

I will use _____ to become a woman of God by using my hands to _____ by _____

Part 5
Key Verse: Isaiah 52:7
How beautiful on the mountains are the feet of those who bring good news, who proclaim peace, who bring good tidings, who proclaim salvation.

I will use _____ to become a woman of God by _____ to those around me."

Part 6
Key Verse: Psalm 46:10
Be still and know that I am God.

I will use _____ to become a woman of God by _____ and _____

Take your "body" home and hang it somewhere in your room (maybe on the back of your door or on your closet.) Each day you see it, be reminded of the different parts of your body and how you can use them to be God's girl each day.

GOT FRUIT?
LEADER GUIDE

MATERIALS NEEDED

- Two-inch key rings
- Colored cardstock cut into quarter-sized cards (nine per student)
- A one-hole punch
- Markers
- One pair of scissors per student

WHAT'S THE POINT?

This lesson is designed to help the students understand what the Fruit of the Spirit are, and that with the Holy Spirit in our lives, we should be displaying these qualities in our lives.

START A DIALOGUE

- Have you ever seen an apple tree? What evidence or information helped you to identify it as an apple tree?
- Have you ever walked by a person and thought to yourself, "That person must be in a band"? Why did you think that?
- Have you ever been around a person and thought to yourself, "That person must be a Christian"? Why did you think that?
- What qualities or characteristics do you think a Christian should have?

Start with the Word
Read Galatians 5:16-26

So I say, live by the Spirit, and you will not gratify the desires of the sinful nature. For the sinful nature desires what is contrary to the Spirit, and the Spirit what is contrary to the sinful nature. They are in conflict with each other, so that you do not do what you want. But if you are led by the Spirit, you are not under law. The acts of the sinful nature are obvious: sexual immorality, impurity and debauchery; idolatry and witchcraft; hatred, discord, jealousy, fits of rage, selfish ambition, dissensions, factions and envy; drunkenness, orgies, and the like. I warn you, as I did before, that those who live like this will not inherit the kingdom of God. But the fruit of the Spirit is love, joy, peace, patience, kindness, goodness, faithfulness, gentleness and self-control. Against such things there is no law. Those who belong to Christ Jesus have crucified the sinful nature with its passions and desires. Since we live by the Spirit, let us keep in step with the Spirit. Let us not become conceited, provoking and envying each other.

GROUP ACTIVITY

As a group, put together a "Fruit of the Spirit" key chain.

Leader Instructions

- Give each student a key ring, markers, a pair of scissors, and an assortment of colored paper (nine sheets each).
- Have each student write "From the Spirit" at the top of each piece of paper.
- On the flip side of that paper, have each student write "Sinful Nature."
- One at time, have your students write each of the "Fruit of the Spirit" on the different colored papers. And on the flip side of each paper, have them write the opposite action or word that corresponds with our sinful nature.

    For example:
    Side 1
    From the Spirit:
    Kindness

Side 2
Sinful Nature:
Hatred

- Take some time to talk about each fruit and its opposite. Ask the student questions listed below to help get discussion going.
- Lastly, have your students punch a hole in the top corner of each piece of "fruit" and attach it to the key ring you provided. Tell them to hang it somewhere that will remind them to display the "Fruit of the Spirit" in their daily life.

Student Instructions

- You will need a key ring, markers, a pair of scissors, and an assortment of multi-colored paper.
- Write "From the Spirit" at the top of each piece of paper.
- On the flip side of that paper, write "Sinful Nature."
- One at time, write each of the "Fruit of the Spirit" on the different colored papers. And on the flip side of each paper, write the opposite action or word that corresponds with our sinful nature (share your example).
- Punch a hole in the top corner of each piece of "fruit" and attach it to the key ring.

 KEEP UP THE DIALOGUE

- What does the Bible mean when it talks about us having a "sinful nature"?
- What does our sinful nature want?
- Who is the Holy Spirit?
- What about those who don't live by the Spirit?
- Why is the sinful man hostile toward God?

HOW DOES THIS APPLY?

- How do we recognize the Holy Spirit's work in our lives?
- What can you do this week to display these qualities in your life?
- How does the Holy Spirit help us to have these qualities in our lives?

TAKE-HOME CHALLENGE

Check out Romans 8:5-8 and Romans 8:9-11 and read what those passages say about living by the Spirit. Let these passages be an encouragement to you this week.

GOT FRUIT?
STUDENT HANDOUT

Read Galatians 5:16-26

So I say, live by the Spirit, and you will not gratify the desires of the sinful nature. For the sinful nature desires what is contrary to the Spirit, and the Spirit what is contrary to the sinful nature. They are in conflict with each other, so that you do not do what you want. But if you are led by the Spirit, you are not under law. The acts of the sinful nature are obvious: sexual immorality, impurity and debauchery; idolatry and witchcraft; hatred, discord, jealousy, fits of rage, selfish ambition, dissensions, factions and envy; drunkenness, orgies, and the like. I warn you, as I did before, that those who live like this will not inherit the kingdom of God. But the fruit of the Spirit is love, joy, peace, patience, kindness, goodness, faithfulness, gentleness and self-control. Against such things there is no law. Those who belong to Christ Jesus have crucified the sinful nature with its passions and desires. Since we live by the Spirit, let us keep in step with the Spirit. Let us not become conceited, provoking and envying each other.

FRUIT OF THE SPIRIT

1.

2.

3.

4.

5.

6.

7.

8.

9.

SINFUL NATURE

SPEND IT. SAVE IT. GIVE IT BACK.
LEADER GUIDE

 MATERIALS NEEDED

- Three containers or Mason jars (per student)
- Black permanent markers
- Large labels (three per student)
- $1 in quarters and nickels, and two $1 bills (for each student)

   (To keep costs down, have students bring the exact change and the containers)

 WHAT'S THE POINT?

God is the source of all we have. He has given us so much to be thankful for, and He is counting on us to take what He has given and use it wisely. In this lesson we are going to focus on managing our money and being good stewards of what God gives us.

Start with the Word
Read 2 Corinthians 9:7-8
You must each decide in your heart how much to give. And don't give reluctantly or in response to pressure. For God loves a person who gives cheerfully. And God will generously provide all you need. Then you will always have everything you need and plenty left over to share with others.

 GROUP ACTIVITY

Talk through "managing money" and being good stewards of what God has given us by utilizing a three-part system. Together create containers/jars that will help students spend, save, and give back their money.

Leader Instructions

- Give each student three containers, a marker, and three labels
- Have students write the following on each of the labels:
  - SPEND IT
  - SAVE IT
  - GIVE IT BACK TO GOD
- Have your students attach one label per jar/container
- Talk through the "DIALOGUE" questions below as a group.

Student Instructions

- You will need three containers and three labels
- Write the following on each of the labels:
  - SPEND IT
  - SAVE IT
  - GIVE IT BACK TO GOD
- Attach one label per jar/container

 START A DIALOGUE

Talk about the following items as they correspond to each jar/container.

Spend It

- How much money (allowance) do you receive each week?
- What types of things do you spend your money on?
- Is it okay to spend money on "stuff"?
- Have you ever spent your money on someone else?
- How do you manage the money you spend?

  Leader Note: Have your students add "It's okay to enjoy what God has given me" on the "SPEND IT" label.

Save It

- Why is it important to save some of our money?
- Is saving money a "strength" or a "weakness" for you?
- What is something that you could save your money for?
- Do you think you would be willing to save 10 percent of your money for future things?

Leader Note: Have your students add "Put something aside for what is to come" on the "SAVE IT" label.

Give It Back to God
Read the following passages that correspond with "Giving to God"
Check out Deuteronomy 14:22-23.
- What is a "tithe"?
- Can we give more than 10 percent?
- By giving, what do we communicate to God?
- Is there a difference between our "tithe" and an "offering"?

Leader Note: God has called us to give 10 percent of what we receive. Your tithe is what you give back to the church (the place you honor God). However, your offering is what you give above and beyond your 10 percent *(example: youth group scholarship fund, support a church missionary, etc.)* The purpose of giving is not to see something in return, but to demonstrate obedience, trust, and love for God.

Check out Matthew 25:14-30
- What happened to the man who was given five talents?
- What happened to the man who was given two talents?
- What happened to the man who was given one talent?
- What is the point of this parable? What is Jesus trying to communicate?

Leader Note: If God can trust you with a little, He will trust with much.

- What should we give back to God?
- When should we give back to God?
- Why should give back to God?
- Would you be willing to try to TITHE each week?

Leader Note: Have your students add "Deuteronomy 14:22-23 and 2 Corinthians 9:7-8" on the "GIVE IT BACK TO GOD" label.

Remember, you can't ever out-give God! Trusting Him with your money now and forming good habits helps you to give more cheerfully and willingly as you get older.

? HOW DOES THIS APPLY?

- Is there anything in your life that is keeping you from trusting God with all that you have?
- How can your leader or a good friend help hold you accountable in this area?

TAKE-HOME CHALLENGE

For Leaders: Help each student get started on their journey toward being a good steward. Give each student $3 to get their containers started. Have each student divide it up as follows. First, place 10 percent in the "GIVE IT BACK TO GOD" container. Then, place 10 percent in the "SAVE IT" container. Last, place the remainder of the money in the "SPEND IT" container.

For Students: Put your jars on your shelf or desk at home. Do your best to utilize the jars as a tool to help you be a good steward of your money on a weekly basis.

SPEND IT. SAVE IT. GIVE IT BACK.
STUDENT HANDOUT

Read 2 Corinthians 9:7-8

You must each decide in your heart how much to give. And don't give reluctantly or in response to pressure. For God loves a person who gives cheerfully. And God will generously provide all you need. Then you will always have everything you need and plenty left over to share with others.

SPEND IT

SAVE IT

GIVE IT BACK TO GOD
Check out Deuteronomy 14:22-23

Check out Matthew 25:14-30

 TAKE-HOME CHALLENGE

Put your jars on your shelf or desk at home. Do your best to utilize the jars as a tool to help you be a good steward of your money on a weekly basis.